Dedicated to my younger self,
I'm finally doing what you
always wanted to accomplish

Planting the Wrong Seeds

Observing people used to be one of my favorite things.
I watched the people that passed me by,
I sat quietly watching interactions take place
but when it came to you
I jumped head first without observing
and I never saw what you were.

Why did I let you have so much power over me?

I wish that I hadn't been blinded
by the idea that someone could love me.
Maybe I would've seen the signals sooner.

Our relationship started before I had a chance to explore.
In the beginning I didn't really mind, because I had never thought about it
but as time went on, I noticed other people more
I became more curious.
I felt the need to explore every option before I was certain what I wanted
but you couldn't let me
because you were too afraid you weren't my answer.

I never should have had to explain myself to you.
No labels are needed
I can be who I want
without having to comfort you
by forcing myself into a box I don't fit in.

You could never just let me have my struggles.
You would never admit that it just sucked in the moment,
someone had it worse or it would get better
but for once I just wanted you to agree.

I started to leave out details when I talked to you.
I left out the best parts of my day,
and I skipped over the funny stories
so you would think I was as miserable as you were.

Behind every kiss
was my raw emotion.
but to you it was a competition
to make me feel
the way you wanted me to.

Did you love me or did you just want to take off my clothes?

I wanted to go explore the world
but you always tried to pull me away.
Was it because you wanted to spend time with me
or to prevent me from seeing you as you really are?

You claimed that you loved me
and I believed you.
But when issues came
that you didn't understand
you just turned angry.

I wish I had known that
sometimes we forget ourselves
because of the potential we see in someone else.
But if we find we have to change who we are at our core
just to keep one person
they shouldn't be in our life.

I always loved games
so you decided to start one.

You always made me the bad guy,
When everything was going good for me.
I was hanging out with my friends more,
I spent more time with my family,
excitement ran through me for the plans I had made,
new hobbies were being explored,
and work was starting to be better,
but I was stil wrong.
Even though you admitted you were the one
that couldn't be happy for me.

Excuses are all I gave you.

I let you change who I was,
because I thought there was potential.
I always gave you the benefit of the doubt,
and I ended up just hating who I turned into.

You were slowly turning into my enemy
as you held me back from what I wanted.
You didn't even notice when I changed,
when everyone else did.

What am I worth?
What place do I have in this world?
Should I feel like this?
Do I deserve to be happy?
You made me question it all.

Looking back,
I should have
listened to my gut.
I had a feeling
that turned out
to be right.

I thought I needed you in my darkest time
but you didn't notice when I was happier
and I deserve so much better.

No emotion I directed at you was undeserved.
I gave you my love,
because I fell for you.
But you also got my anger and distaste
for the things you projected on me
and how you blamed me.

It was never me
or what I couldn't give you.
It was your inability to let go of your expectations.

I thought you were a flower
I could let grow in my garden
but it turns out you were a weed.

Watered with Darkness

What mark am I leaving on the world?
Will people remember when I'm gone?
Is this how I want to be remembered?
Who will miss me?

Nobody ever listened to me.
I just needed exercise
or to get off my phone,
sleep better,
or eat better.
They didn't even listen when my pain became physical.
I slept on the couch for days,
barely getting up.
But it took the hospital for someone to finally give a fuck.

They told me I was a trooper.
That I was strong.
That I got through it.
But what about the struggles they couldn't see?
Then I was just emotional,
I was doing everything wrong.
Why couldn't they see it then?

I felt like a disappointment,
I felt like a failure,
I didn't want to feel that way anymore
but the depression was pushing me back into bed.

If you asked me what my life was like
I wouldn't really know what to tell you.
Of course there's the highs, on top of the world
but also the lows,
spending the night crying alone.
I always feel sad and tired and empty
but if she knew, she'd come to hold me and love me,
but would they?
I think that's what hurts the most,
not knowing
Would they?
Would they care?
Would they even notice?
When I started taking longer showers
because I would sit down
ready to give up.
Or would they call me emotional?
Or say that I'm fine?
But when you feel that way
you know that you're not fine
because even just having to get out of bed
is enough reason to cry.

Why did my brain forget everything I wanted?
What happened to wanting to skydive?
What happened to traveling the world?
What happened to the tiny creatures I wanted to create?
Depression told me that it wasn't worth it,
that nothing could make it better.

I couldn't even look at myself.
I avoided mirrors,
I thought I was ugly,
unlovable
but I just didn't see the beauty under the surface.

I wish I was a girl
with no issues or pain,
I often saw the problems
as a thing to hide away.
I had to be strong
And push it all down,
I never got help
and I always broke down.
Trying to find a way to let myself breathe
without letting me drown in my tear created sea.
I could do it on my own
I thought I'd get better.
Turns out, shutting down
makes it all sadder.
Just living was hard
with no friends around,
I pushed them all away
with the feelings I pushed out.

Everytime I crawled into bed,
The darkness seeped in again
Like the night was filling me up.

What are you afraid of?
Spiders?
Sharks?
Death?
It used to be.
Now it's letting it get bad again,
crying myself to sleep,
not wanting to get out of bed,
not letting anyone know.
But sometimes it seems so easy
to just let go.

There was always an expectation to be happy
no matter the circumstances or the situation.
But not everything was exciting
or appealing as expected.
I just want someone to agree.

Tears pooled in the fabric of my pillow case,
my eyes grew heavy with exhaustion
and my mind became tired of running.

There was no one in my life that knew.
I was seemingly normal during the day
I made jokes,
smiled,
laughed
but when I was alone
in the darkness
everything fell apart.

I couldn't see the light at the end of the tunnel,
I could only feel the darkness pressing around me.
I couldn't see the end, or how it could get better.
So I just cried,
every night
until I ran out of tears.

Sometimes life gets overwhelmingly hard,
there's so many things to blame it on,
so many opportunities to brush it all off.
But one day it will all come back
crushing down on top of you all at once.
Trying to forget doesn't make it easier
but in the moment,
it makes you feel better.

As a child, I always took charge.
I was the one who started the game,
I was the one to lead projects,
I always volunteered to help,
and that was something I never let you take away.
I never wanted to die,
but I quit caring.
I still had dreams and aspirations,
but they all seemed unattainable.
I planned to just coast
until one day I got there.

My legs were stiff,
My body was heavy,
I couldn't breathe
and every time I woke up
panic filled me.

I wanted to push away the feelings,
I wanted to go back to feeling happy,
I wanted to feel like myself again.
But when I ignored the feelings
they hit me all at once,
so much harder.

Lungs restricted,
heavy limbs
waterlogged brain,
aching heart,
left at the bottom of the ocean
but I wouldn't feel like this forever.

I was lost
but I was just under the surface,
waiting to burst free at my first chance.

Petals Falling

There were parts of you I could never understand,
but I still supported you.
Why couldn't you do the same for me?

Pill bottles don't create happiness,
they create a distraction.

Nobody ever told me.
Almost two years
and not a soul told me.

I thought that I could and should fix you
but it's impossible.
I couldn't force you to change
and I broke myself trying.

I so desperately wanted to be happy.
Not for anyone else
but for me,
because I felt so much better.
I was finally getting there
until I was around you.

I had nothing,
I was sad and miserable
and you were the one thing I had going for me.
But you were also contributing to my sadness,
I didn't want to let you go
because I didn't want all the lights to go out.
But I had to
to let in the sun.

Feeling trapped has always been a pet peeve.
But being with you slowly put me in a straight jacket.
My arms were held down,
it got hard to breathe
until finally I had to bust out.

Not having control over anything in my life,
I did the only thing I could
to get my happiness back
and that was getting out of your grasp.

Respectful and kind were things I had always been to you
I never cheated, or lied about anyone else
just kept a separate life that was balanced and healthy from you.
Finally things were going good for me,
but you couldn't accept that,
so I had to leave.

Without control over your movement forward
we felt like a ticking time bomb.
No matter what I identified in you,
a change wouldn't happen.
You were only happy when things were good
but crumpled the moment I brought up anything.
I had thought about leaving you,
But I was scared of the risk.
Until you blew up and I knew it was over.

Sometimes I thought there wouldn't be an after you
but towards the end it seemed like the only option.

I wanted to chase my dreams
but I couldn't with you
until I realized
if you cared
you would have let me go.
If we were the right match,
we would find our way back
because nothing important can be lost.

I gave up myself like I always did.
I skipped meals,
I stopped sleeping,
I cried everyday
constantly worried I was making a mistake.

I hated that I let myself cry for you
because you brought me so much pain.

No matter how many distractions you have,
the feelings will still be there.
Once the distractions go away
it will all hit you at once.

We always take the people in our life for granted
until they are threatened to be taken away.
We forget that we only have so much time,
then everything we know ends.

It's always easy to say goodbye
until you don't know if it's the last.

She sat quietly across from me
listening to what I had to say
and she started to see
why I couldn't stay.

I don't resent you
but I get angry when I remember everything you did
the hurt you brought me,
how you held me back from my dreams
But you helped me grow
leaving a bittersweet taste on my tongue.

I cannot take anymore hurt in my life.

She grabbed my hand and pulled me close
but it had been too soon after you.
For some reason I felt guilty
like I was cheating on you
even though we were no longer together.
I held her hand anyway
trying to forget the feel of yours.

I ran away from everything I knew,
sinking down with my head in my hands
on a street I didn't know
and then she came
and wrapped her arms around me
holding me close
while I cried into her chest.

Is there someone else?
I imagined it so much differently.
I wanted you to find happiness,
I would be happy for you.
But when I thought you moved on
I was overcome by how sad I was,
even though it wasn't our time.

Ripping My Roots

I tried so hard to continue on with my life
but all I could think about was you.
You set up camp in my mind
and no matter how much I tried
you wouldn't take down your tent.

Surgeons couldn't fix my broken heart like they could my other wounds.

I blamed myself for everything
even though I gave you my all
through everything we went through.
And when I finally chose me
you couldn't handle it.

Even though we aren't together anymore
I still would have given up anything
to take away your pain.

I never blamed you.
I even told you it was not your fault,
I took all of the responsibility,
because it really was my choice.
But you still blamed me for your own choices.

Why do I still care?
Will I always be terrified of losing you?
Can I ever let go?
How long will I feel nauseous at the thought of you being mad at me?
When will I stop losing sleep over intrusive thoughts of your words?

I wish I could sprout wings and fly away.
Then I wouldn't be so worried about your existence.

I sat in my car
holding my breath
stiff as can be.
I watched as the car passed,
driving through the parking lot
while I hoped it wasn't you.
I hid behind every car
as the same one you had driven passed.
I ducked into the next aisle at the store
hoping you wouldn't be around the corner.
Everywhere I went
I was afraid you would pop up.

All I saw was your pale lifeless body. Laying there limply while tears streaked my face. People and sounds swarmed around me but I could only hear the sound of my sobs. I desperately wanted to hold you against me and feel your heartbeat again. But instead warm arms wrapped around behind me, pulling me away from you.

Looking out at all the faces watching me
I got nervous.
What was the right thing to say?
Who you pretended to be?
Or who you really were?
I sucked in a breath
before I started my speech.

I started having nightmares.
At first it was only about me,
I would be trapped in a fire.
I would fall and not be able to get up.
But when I heard what happened
in the rare moments I got sleep,
I woke up crying at the image of your funeral
I saw your lifeless body
And I was petrified.

You came up behind me
wrapping your arms around my waist
I turned and saw your face.
You leaned in trying to kiss me
even though I said no
I turned my face away
struggling against you.
You pinned my arms down
covered my mouth
stifling my attempted screams.
Until I sat up startled
with tears falling in streams.

You tell me conflicting things
and I don't even know what you want from me anymore.

I want to go back
to when all that mattered
was which princess I would be.

Just because we had happy memories
didn't mean we were happy.
We were more than toxic together
but sometimes I would forget,
remembering the soft touch
of your hands on my skin.

I didn't let you have everything
and in some ways I'm glad
but I regret letting you have as much as you did.

Desperate to end my pain
I tried to be your friend
but was only met with my scars.

It took me weeks to forgive myself
for what you did.
But that's exactly what it was,
your choice.
And nothing I did differently
would've changed your mind.

No matter what you say,
it wasn't my fault.
I did nothing wrong.
I did everything I could.
And I'm a better person
now because of it.

I built myself up
after we broke up
but you still expected me to be there
when you started to feel the fear.

I spent my time petrified
by the thought of losing you.
You aren't mine anymore
but that doesn't mean I don't love you.

Behind every door
I hoped to find a fairytale land
that would help me forget your memory.

Growing up I always had the biggest imagination.
Reading every fantasy story I could get my hands on,
telling my friends stories about ladybug families,
playing teacher and house,
writing my own fictional stories
but my creativity diminished as I grew older.
Now I wished I still had other worlds in my brain
so I could escape the one with you in it.

Love and misery,
conflicting emotions when you think of me.

It seemed like you didn't truly want to get better,
you held yourself in your miserable state.
When I was making progess
you no longer seemed to understand me
because I was finally at a different stage.

Sometimes I got close
to letting my intrusive thoughts take over.
But I knew any of those actions would hurt you,
and I never wanted to do that to you,
even though I felt like I was always bleeding out,
from all your stabs.

Sleep was lost,
meals were skipped
and tears were shed.
All for you to say I didn't care.

Fantasizing about running away,
finding a new place to seek isolation.
I wouldn't worry about you showing up
and I wouldn't have to run from my misery.

I'm terrified
I won't know how to love again.
If someone touches me in the soft ways you did
I think I might just burst into tears.

I feel like an addict,
counting the days I've been sober from you.

I told you I had no one.
You retorted that I had you.
I didn't mean I didn't have anyone,
I meant I had no one to share the details of my life with.
When I needed help, I had it
but nobody wanted to hear about the miniscule moments of my day.

I miss the memories of what we used to be.
The way you could make me laugh,
and how you always wanted to hold my hand
but I don't miss you anymore.

I carried the weight of it all.
It wasn't my decision
but I blamed myself anyway.
I carried the universe on my shoulders
but I'm finally starting to let go.

Blooming

Seeking acceptance,
I hid what I truly wanted.
But it turns out,
I'm the only one
that can dictate my happiness.

The best decision isn't always the easiest.
Sometimes the hardest things,
are the best for us.

There's so much I want to accomplish,
getting married,
having a baby of my own,
finally being able to say I have a job I love,
traveling to everywhere I can
and experiencing at least one movie moment.
They are the reason I fight to keep from drowning
when the waves get too big.

Doing the right thing
does not
make you the bad guy.

I don't want my life to end in disappointment.
I don't want it to end feeling this way.
I don't want to be remembered because of this.
I want to write my own story,
so I will find something better to fill the next chapter.

I never spoke up for myself,
I let you walk all over me,
I forgot my worth,
I questioned who I was,
I didn't believe in my potential,
when I should have remembered
that I am the only one
that can decide what I can accomplish.

I didn't see the change at first.
It was slow and took a year.
But I could finally smile more
than I cried at night
and the weight seemed to be gone.

I was growing
with
or without you.

After surviving the darkest depression,
I feel invincible.
I can and will overcome anything thrown my way.

I left you to search for the good
that you couldn't give me.

I was worried you told your family lies
like you spewed our whole relationship
but I was embraced and loved.

Happily she let me in.
She hugged me,
told me everything was ok
and knew I was doing the right thing.

She told me I wasn't the bad guy.
I did the right thing,
even if you blamed me for your pain.

I wanted to rush what was to come
until I realized,
then the end wouldn't be as sweet.

Can I rid you of me with change?
Striving to become a better person
and surrounded by better people,
so much change that you wouldn't even recognize me?

I go through each day
giving it my all
because I refuse to let you win.

It's a constant battle in my head
to figure out what the right thing is.
But at the end of the day
I feel better with distance.

Without you I could fill my life with good.
Good friends,
good memories
and happiness.

When we were together I took life for granted
Until I realized I didn't like the way that felt.
When I got my space I started to appreciate everything,
the sunrise I saw every morning,
the flowers lining the sidewalks,
the excitement my dog has when I come home after a long day.
Now I try to capture everything I want to remember and appreciate,
even if it means a million pictures of the same mountains.

After you I changed.
Instead of watching the bright moon when I couldn't sleep
I watched the sun rise with excitement for the new adventures I would face.

I love dancing around in my room by myself,
singing to the music too loud when nobody is home,
painting my nails pale pink
and braiding my hair.
I love watching the sunrise,
jumping into the pool for the first time in the summer
and licking the spoon clean of brownie batter.
I love traveling,
people watching,
reading about imaginary places,
and hearing babies giggle.
And I refuse to give up until I have experienced everything else.

I think I've hit a new point in my life.
The demons in my head no longer scare me,
I choose to fight them
rather than letting them take control again.
The real world has enough monsters
I don't want to worry about my own mind too.

It felt so good to be free
without the burdens put on me
and the guilt for others actions.

Rather than filling myself with drugs
that pretend to bring happiness,
I turned to laughter,
sunsets,
music,
books,
friends,
anything I could find to fill the void you never could
Everyone told me time was what I needed,
but time didn't do much.
It was the people I surrounded myself with
and the joy I found doing what I love.

I don't care if it matters to you.
I have dreams
and I will chase them.

I had too many surgeries and too much time taken from me to give up.
I will continue until every bucket list item is completed.

You and your happiness
should always be your number one priority.

You might move on to someone new sooner
but I will be strong,
more confident,
successful,
and satisfied
with the life I build after I you.

The sun rose today
and so will I.
Radiating the same brightness,
to keep away the darkness
trying to crawl back up my throat.

I won't lose myself anymore.
The only thing that will go away
is my fear and doubt.

I'm here today
and I'm so grateful.

I have so many things I want to do in my life,
but after all it's all about the climb right?
So until then I'm going to enjoy the journey
and I'm going to appreciate the view at every peak.

Each day was a small victory for me.
Thinking about you a little less,
reaching out to you less often,
feeling happier bit by bit
and slowly mending my heart.

1/24
I could finally,
truthfully,
unapologetically
say that I was great.

Wildness will always run through me.
From the natural unruly pattern of waves through my hair,
the desire to run rampant across the world,
accomplishing every crazy thing I can muster
and spontaneously filling my skin with ink.
Yet I will always seek asylum in the quiet
the comfort of my bed,
the darkness of the room,
the comfort of her arms
where I can finally relax.

I'm glad I never gave up.

Life is short.
Don't pass up the opportunity to pick up rocks on a trial,
or watch the sunset out the window,
eat your favorite meal,
take the trip you've been longing for
and get the tattoo you love.

I never had an consistent answer for the question,
who do you want to be when you grow up?
At one point it was a teacher,
a gymnast
or even an engineer
but I never really had a passion.
Now all I can think about is how amazing the future will be
not because I know where I'm going,
but because I'll be happy.

Instead of being sad
I decided I would bloom.
I wouldn't cry late at night anymore
but plant my feet
and reach for the stars.

www.ingramcontent.com/pod-product-compliance
Lightning Source LLC
Chambersburg PA
CBHW060325050426
42449CB00011B/2654